DUCKS, GEESE & SWANS

Created and Written by

John Bonnett Wexo

Zoological Consultant

Charles R. Schroeder, D.V.M.

Director Emeritus
San Diego Zoo &
San Diego Wild Animal Park

Scientific Consultants

Jean Delacour, Ph. D.

Director Emeritus
Los Angeles County Museum
of Natural History

W. Scott Drieschman

Curator of Birds
Sea World, Inc.

Paul A. Johnsgard, Ph. D.

School of Life Sciences
University of Nebraska

Frank S. Todd

Corporate Curator of Birds
Sea World, Inc.

Creative Education

Published by Creative Education, Inc., 123 South Broad Street, Mankato, Minnesota 56001

Printed by permission of Wildlife Education, Ltd.

ISBN 0-88682-224-6

Contents

Ducks, Geese & Swans are called the waterfowl in the United States and the wildfowl in England. But no matter what they are called, they are one of the world's most beautiful and impressive groups of birds. And it's easy to see why so many people love them.

As a group, waterfowl combine most of the things that people love about birds in general. Ducks, geese, and swans are often brightly colored and boldly patterned. They are usually wonderful fliers. And they have a wide variety of behaviors that can be fascinating to watch.

Indeed, the sheer variety of sizes, shapes, colors, and behaviors among the waterfowl is astonishing. The smallest member of the group is the Pygmy goose of Africa. This bird is less than a foot long (30 centimeters) and weighs only a little more than half a pound (285 grams). The largest of the waterfowl is more than *60 times* larger. It is the magnificent Trumpeter swan, which can weigh more than 40 pounds (18 kilograms) and have a wingspan of more than 8 feet (2.4 meters).

Among the waterfowl, the most brilliantly colored birds are the ducks. And some of them are famous for the dazzling colors they display. The Wood duck (shown on the cover of this book) is certainly one of the most beautiful birds on earth. And there are dozens of other ducks that are just as beautifully colored.

Many types of waterfowl like to gather together in large groups (as the Black swans at right are doing). At times, there may be thousands of ducks, geese or swans gathered in a single place. And when they take to the air all at once, it is one of the most exciting events in the natural world.

A large part of the popularity of waterfowl has to do with the fact that they are easier to see than many other types of birds. You may have to climb to the top of a high mountain to see an eagle, or sail to the ends of the earth to see a penguin. But you can often see waterfowl by simply looking out your window. Many live in the same areas as humans, and the main migration routes of some birds pass right over major centers of human population. Millions of people get a chance every year to see waterfowl and admire them.

Waterfowl can often have surprising colors. Most people think that swans are white. But there are swans in Australia and New Zealand that are coal black, with bright red bills.

4

The best way to tell if a bird is a duck, a goose, or a swan is to look at its bill. In general, the members of each waterfowl group have a bill shape that is different from the other groups.

As a rule, ducks have rather long bills that are wide and flat. Geese have bills that are shorter and more rounded. And swan bills are half way between the other two in their shape.

The different bill shapes are related to the different kinds of foods the birds eat, as you will see on these pages.

Swans like to feed on plants that grow under the water. They rip the plants up or bite them off. To help them do this, they have bills that are thick and strong. The long necks of swans often make it possible for them to get food without diving. They can just reach down into the water and bite off the plants they want.

The bills of mergansers are very different from the bills of all other waterfowl. This is because mergansers use their bills for catching fish most of the time. The bills are long and thin with tooth-like serrations along the edges. When a merganser grabs a slippery fish, the serrations hook into it and keep it from getting away.

Most waterfowl will dive for food from time to time. But mergansers and other sea ducks do the most diving.

HOODED MERGANSER
Mergus cucullatus

Some waterfowl have crests on their heads that they can raise or lower. This merganser has its hood up. When it dives, it will flatten the hood against its head.

MERGANSER

SWAN

All waterfowl have thick bodies with rather short and thick legs. The feet are always webbed, although some types of waterfowl have more webbing than others.

BLACK SWAN
Cygnus atratus

Most waterfowl have hooks on the end of their bills that look like fingernails. For this reason, the hooks are called "nails."

Geese like to eat grass and other plants, and their bills are ideal for this purpose. The bills are very sturdy, so the geese can easily tear off clumps of grass. The serrations inside the bill are used to cut the grass up before it is swallowed.

MAGELLAN GOOSE
Chloephaga picta

GOOSE

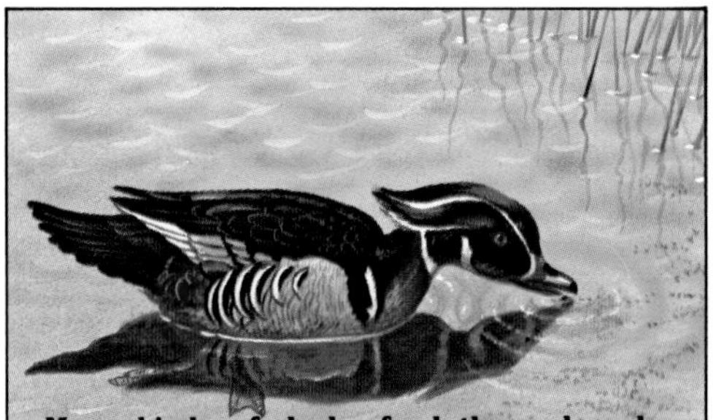

Many kinds of ducks feed themselves by sifting tiny bits of food out of the water. This method of getting food is called dabbling, and the ducks that do it are called Dabbling Ducks. The ducks swim along with their mouths open, and let water flow into their bills. The serrations in the bill scoop the food out of the water, as shown below. Dabbling Ducks eat almost anything that floats into their mouths—seeds, water weed, and many other things.

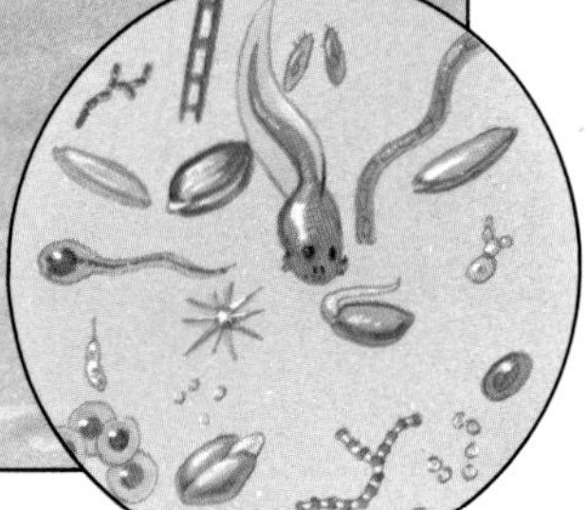

WOOD DUCK
Aix sponsa

DUCK

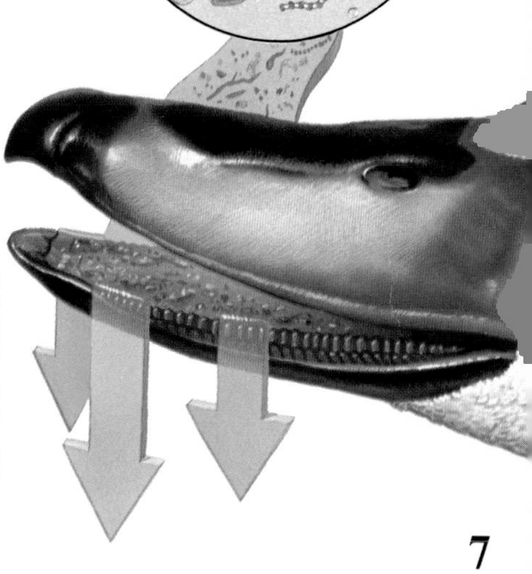

Dabbling ducks must strain many gallons of water to get the food they need. The water and food flow into the bill together. The serrations catch the food, and the water flows out of the mouth.

7

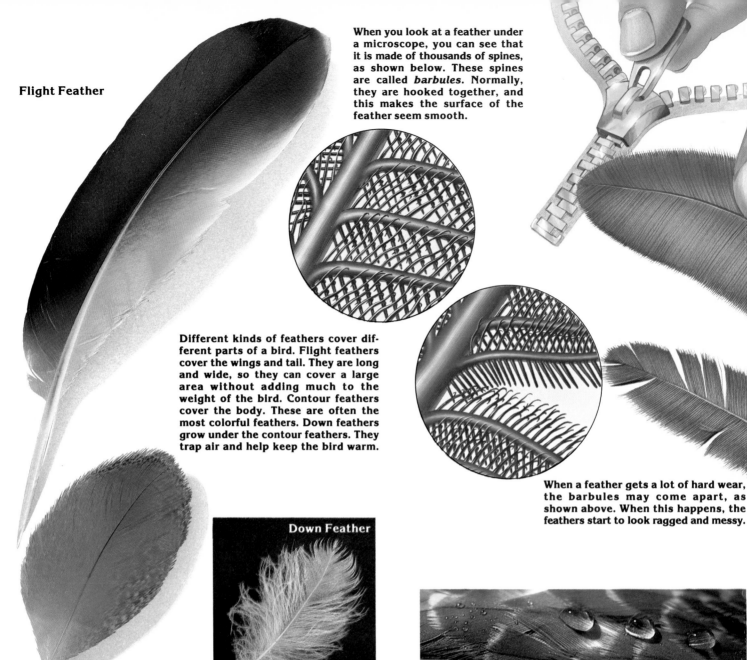

Flight Feather

When you look at a feather under a microscope, you can see that it is made of thousands of spines, as shown below. These spines are called *barbules*. Normally, they are hooked together, and this makes the surface of the feather seem smooth.

Different kinds of feathers cover different parts of a bird. Flight feathers cover the wings and tail. They are long and wide, so they can cover a large area without adding much to the weight of the bird. Contour feathers cover the body. These are often the most colorful feathers. Down feathers grow under the contour feathers. They trap air and help keep the bird warm.

When a feather gets a lot of hard wear, the barbules may come apart, as shown above. When this happens, the feathers start to look ragged and messy.

Down Feather

Contour Feather

Feathers are very important in the lives of all ducks, geese, and swans. They provide an outer covering for the bodies of the birds that helps to keep them warm. Without this covering, many waterfowl that live in cold places would freeze to death.

Waterfowl feathers also make the birds waterproof. And the importance of this is obvious for birds that spend a great deal of time in the water.

Finally, it is the feathers of waterfowl that make some of them so beautiful. And this beauty is very important for the survival of some waterfowl, as you will see on these pages.

As everybody knows, water runs off a duck's back. And it also runs off the backs of geese and swans. This is because the feathers have oil on them, and this makes them waterproof. By helping to keep water out, the oil helps to keep waterfowl dry and warm.

8

MANDARIN DUCK
Aix galericulata

PYGMY GOOSE
Nettapus auritus

COMB DUCK
Sarkidiornis melanotos melanotos

EUROPEAN SCAUP
Aythya marila marila

CANVASBACK DUCK
Aythya valisineria

ROSYBILL
Netta peposaca

RED-CRESTED POCHARD
Netta rufina

MAGELLANIC GOOSE
Chloephaga picta

WHOOPER SWAN
Cygnus cygnus cygnus

RUDDY SHELDUCK
Tadorna ferruginea

ANDEAN GOOSE
Chloephaga melanoptera

EUROPEAN EIDER
Somateria mollissima mollissima

ASHY-HEADED GOOSE
Chloephaga poliocephala

ORINOCO GOOSE
Neochen jubatus

STELLER'S EIDER
Polysticta stelleri

KING EIDER
Somateria spectabilis

COMMON SHELDUCK
Tadorna tadorna

RADJAH SHELDUCK
Tadorna radjah

EGYPTIAN GOOSE
Alopochen aegyptiacus

A bird can repair its feathers by re-hooking the barbules. It can use its bill to zip up each row of barbules, in a way that is similar to zipping a zipper. This is called *preening*. As it preens, the bird also cleans the feathers.

There can be an astonishing number of feathers on waterfowl. Naturally enough, smaller birds have fewer feathers than larger birds. A Green-winged teal may have only 11,500 feathers—but a Whistling swan can have over 25,000 feathers. There may be more than *15,000 feathers* on the neck alone!

WHISTLING SWAN

Waterfowl spend a lot of time preening. They carefully zip up the barbules in each feather and put a thin coat of oil on many of the feathers. The oil comes from a special gland, and they use their bills to spread it on the feathers. Sometimes, the birds have to get into some strange positions to reach all of their feathers.

WHOOPER SWAN

As a rule, male ducks have brighter feathers than females. This is because females must sit on nests to hatch eggs—and they are safer if predators can't see them. The dark colors and camouflage patterns on most females can make them very hard to see, even at close distance. Sometimes, the males use their bright colors to protect the females. When a predator comes close to the nest, a male may fly into the air, as shown above. He may make a lot of noise and try to make the predator follow him away from the nest. If the predator does go after the male, the female and her precious eggs will be safe.

ORINOCO GEESE

With geese, the males and females of each species often look very much like each other. And this is also true of swans. The males are usually larger than the females, but otherwise it is hard to tell them apart.

MANDARIN DUCK

Some ducks can leap into flight with great speed. It is no easy matter for an Arctic fox to catch a fleeing Spectacled eider.

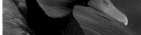

RED-CRESTED POCHARD

Bright colors help male ducks to attract females during the breeding season, and this is probably the main reason why ducks are so colorful. Some birds are so gaudy that it almost looks like somebody painted them with a brush. Wonderful colors are often combined with intricate patterns, as shown above.

Female Plumage

After the breeding season is over, male ducks sometimes molt their bright feathers. And when new feathers grow in, they may look like female feathers. The new coat of feathers is called an *eclipse plumage*, and it can make a male as hard to see as a female. This is good for males because it makes it more difficult for predators to catch them. Males may stay in eclipse plumage until a new breeding season begins. Then they molt again and get a new coat of bright feathers.

Male Eclipse Plumage

After a time, feathers wear out and cannot be repaired anymore. For this reason, all waterfowl shed their feathers at certain times and get new ones. This is called *molting*. Most ducks shed their body feathers twice a year, and wing feathers only once a year.

Male Breeding Plumage

The beauty and variety of waterfowl seem almost endless. There are 147 living species of ducks, geese, and swans in the world—and more than half of them have magnificent colors and patterns that are a wonder to behold. On these pages, you'll find 70 of the most beautiful members of the family. All birds shown are males in breeding plumage.

STIFF-TAILS

MUSK DUCK
Biziura lobata

RUDDY DUCK
Oxyura jamaicensis

EMPEROR GOOSE
Anser canagicus

WHITEFRONT GOOSE
Anser albifrons

BARNACLE GOOSE
Branta leucopsis

SNOW GOOSE
Anser caerulescens

CANADA GOOSE
Branta canadensis

HAWAIIAN GOOSE
Branta sandvicensis

RED-BREASTED GOOSE
Branta ruficollis

BAR-HEADED GOOSE
Anser indicus

GRAYLAG GOOSE
Anser anser

TRUE GEESE

SPUR-WINGED GOOSE
Plectropterus gambensis gambensis

WOOD DUCK
Aix sponsa

MANED GOOSE
Chenonetta jubata

EIDERS

SPECTACLED EIDER
Somateria fischeri

10

Flying is something that most waterfowl do very well. In fact, many species are famous for the long migrations they make every year. Migrating waterfowl may travel thousands of miles to reach good sources of food and good places to raise their young.

To guide them during these long flights, many waterfowl use methods of navigation that scientists don't yet fully understand. The birds use the sun and stars—and possibly other means—to find their way, as explained at right.

Some scientists think that waterfowl use the earth's magnetic field to help them find their way—in the same way that people use compasses.

TRUMPETER SWANS

Almost everybody has seen waterfowl flying in a "V" formation, like a squadron of airplanes. The birds may do this to avoid crashing into each other in the air. As they fly, they "talk" to each other by honking, quacking, and making other noises. This helps to keep the members of a flock together, even in dense clouds or at night. Each member of the flock can always hear where the others are. When swans and geese fly, they usually hold their long necks straight out in front of them.

After they arrive in the north, the geese build nests and lay eggs. They seem to time the laying of the eggs so that they will hatch when the days are longest and the weather is warmest. In this way, the geese give their young a better chance of surviving.

Let's follow some Canada geese as they make their yearly migrations. The cycle starts in the spring, when the geese leave their wintering ground and head north. They may fly in huge flocks.

WHITE-FACED TREE DUCK
Dendrocygna viduata

HOODED MERGANSER
Mergus cucullatus

PERUVIAN TORRENT DUCK
Merganetta armata leucogenis

MERGANSERS

RED-CRESTED MERGANSER
Mergus serrator serrator

BLACK-BELLIED TREE DUCK
Dendrocygna autumnalis

TORRENT DUCKS

SMEW
Mergus albellus

MALLARD
Anas platyrhynchos

BLUE DUCK
Hymenolaimus malacorhynchos

CHILOE WIDGEON
Anas sibilatrix

PINTAIL DUCK
Anas acuta

**NEW ZEALAND
BROWN DUCK**
Anas aucklandica

GREATER BAHAMA PINTAIL
Anas bahamensis rubirostris

PRAIRIE BLUE-WINGED TEAL
Anas discors discors

CAPE TEAL
Anas capensis

**CINNAMON
TEAL**
Anas cyanoptera

PHILIPPINE DUCK
Anas luzonica

PINK-EARED DUCK
Malacorhynchus membranaceus

NEW ZEALAND SHOVELLER
Anas rhynchotis variegata

BAIKAL TEAL
Anas formosa

ARGENTINE RED SHOVELLER
Anas platalea

DABBLING DUCKS

FALCATED DUCK
Anas falcata

RINGED TEAL
Calonetta leucophrys

11

BUFFLEHEAD
Bucephala albeola

LONG-TAILED DUCK
Clangula hyemalis

HARLEQUIN DUCK
Histrionicus histrionicus

SURF SCOTER
Melanitta perspicillata

SEA DUCKS

AMERICAN BLACK SCOTER
Melanitta nigra americana

BARROW'S GOLDENEYE
Bucephala islandica

PLUMED TREE DUCK
Dendrocygna eytoni

BLACK SWAN
Cygnus atratus

TREE DUCKS

TRUMPETER SWAN
Cygnus cygnus buccinator

SWANS

CAPE BARREN GOOSE
Cereopsis novae-hollandiae

BLACK-NECKED SWAN
Cygnus melanocoryphus

COSCOROBA SWAN
Coscoroba coscoroba

MUTE SWAN
Cygnus olor

FLIGHTLESS STEAMER DUCK
Tachyeres brachypterus

Waterfowl seem able to use the position of the sun in the sky to tell them where they are. Like the pilots of long-distance airplanes, they may use the sun to make sure they are flying in the right direction.

When they get close to their destination, the birds may use local landmarks to guide them for the final miles, as the Canada goose below is doing. This is similar to the way that you use familiar buildings and streets to find your way home. But waterfowl use rivers, mountains, and other natural landmarks instead.

Some waterfowl may fly night and day when they migrate. At night, they probably use the positions of the stars in the sky to guide them, as human sailors do. This is a very complex thing for people to do, and it is amazing that these birds can do it.

It usually takes about 27 days before the young geese hatch from the eggs. Unlike many other birds, waterfowl chicks hatch with their eyes open and they are covered with downy feathers.

Unlike most other birds, waterfowl adults do not bring food to their young in the nest. Within hours after they hatch, the baby birds are able to swim and dive—and find their own food.

JULY   AUGUST   SEPTEMBER   OCTOBER

In the far north, the summer may be very short. For this reason, birds that are hatched in the north must grow fast. They must be ready to fly south when the cold weather comes. Young Ross's geese are ready to fly when they are only *40 days old.*

ROSS'S GOOSE

When waterfowl migrate, they use specific routes—"highways in the sky" that are called *flyways*. In North America, there are four main flyways, as shown at left. Different groups of waterfowl all have their own routes. They use the same routes to fly north in the spring and south in the fall. Some of the flyways have been used by waterfowl for an incredibly long time—perhaps more than a million years.

MALLARD

In the fall, *100 million* waterfowl move down out of Canada and Alaska to spend the winter in warmer places. Many of them stop in the southern United States, but large numbers go on to Central and South America. When they make these long journeys, most waterfowl stop to feed and rest from time to time. But some species may fly more than 2,000 miles (3,219 kilometers) without stopping.

The first feathers of the chicks often have camouflage patterns on them. This makes it harder for predators to see them. As the young birds grow up, they molt these baby feathers and begin to look more like their parents.

CACKLING GOOSE

Some waterfowl have been known to migrate more than 7,000 miles (11,265 kilometers), from Canada to South America. When waterfowl migrate over long distances, they sometimes fly very high and very fast. Some of them fly more than 5 miles up in the air (8 kilometers). And they may go faster than 50 miles per hour (80 kilometers per hour).

The young geese eat a lot and grow fast. As summer comes to an end, the weather starts turning colder. By this time, the young are large enough and strong enough to fly. As snow begins to cover the ground, they take to the air and join their parents on the long voyage south.

At the end of their flight, the geese land on their wintering grounds. Here, they will spend the winter, eating and growing fat—getting ready for the spring and their next migration north.

NOVEMBER   DECEMBER   JANUARY   FEBRUARY   **13**

The Water is a favorite place for waterfowl, and they are usually more comfortable in the water than they are on land. Almost all ducks, geese and swans spend a great deal of time in the water or close to it. They are all excellent swimmers. And some are also wonderful divers. As a rule, geese spend more time on land than other waterfowl—but even they can swim well, and dive if necessary.

There are two main reasons why waterfowl stay close to water. They find most of their food in water—and they can use it as a place to escape from predators.

SURF SCOTER

Sea ducks may spend months at sea, without coming in sight of land. Like penguins, they have special glands that remove salt from the water they drink and the food they eat. The liquid salt runs down the bill and drips off the end.

KING EIDER
Somateria spectabilis

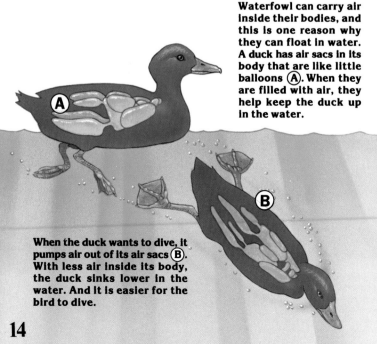

Waterfowl can carry air inside their bodies, and this is one reason why they can float in water. A duck has air sacs in its body that are like little balloons (A). When they are filled with air, they help keep the duck up in the water.

When the duck wants to dive, it pumps air out of its air sacs (B). With less air inside its body, the duck sinks lower in the water. And it is easier for the bird to dive.

SEE FOR YOURSELF how the air sacs inside a duck can help it to float or dive. Get two balloons and fill one with air. Put both balloons in water and try to push them under. The balloon with air is hard to sink, like a duck with its air sacs filled. The other balloon goes under easily, like a duck without air sacs.

14

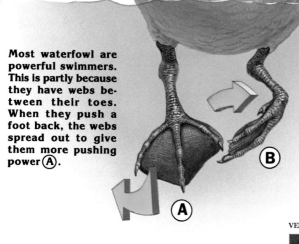

Most waterfowl are powerful swimmers. This is partly because they have webs between their toes. When they push a foot back, the webs spread out to give them more pushing power Ⓐ.

The foot folds up as it moves forward again Ⓑ. If the webs stayed open, they would drag through the water too much and slow the bird down.

COMB DUCK

Quite a few waterfowl have fancy ornaments and bright colors on their heads. These can often be seen when the birds are swimming in the water, even at a distance. And they may help males to attract females. Some birds have large lumps on their bills, and many have brightly colored bills.

When ducks dive, they usually don't go down more than 10 or 20 feet (3 to 6 meters). But some ducks can dive much deeper. King eiders may go down 180 feet or more (55 meters) to feed on sea urchins and other sea creatures. Diving ducks have very large feet to give them more swimming power.

VERSICOLOR TEAL

ROSYBILL POCHARD

MUSCOVY DUCK

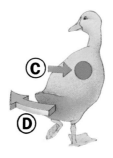

With the next step, everything happens in the opposite direction. The body swings one way Ⓐ and the tail swings the other Ⓑ. This is what we call a waddle.

Because its legs are so far apart, the duck must shift its weight a good distance Ⓐ every time it takes a step. This causes the tail to swing far in the opposite direction Ⓑ.

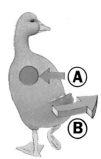

In general, the best swimmers among the waterfowl are the most awkward members of the group on land. This is because the best swimmers have their legs placed far back on their bodies. This gives them more power for swimming—but it makes it harder for them to walk on land. With so much of their weight in front of their legs, they have to walk very carefully to avoid falling over on their faces.

Ducks and other waterfowl waddle because their legs are short and are placed rather far apart on their bodies. When a duck walks, it must shift most of its body weight over the foot that is hitting the ground, or it will lose its balance.

15

The future of waterfowl will depend on the actions of people. Like all wild animals, they must live in a world that people are changing in many ways. If people make the wrong changes, the future of waterfowl (and most other wild animals) will be very bad.

The main threat to ducks, geese and swans is the destruction of their habitats — the places they need for breeding and living. Unfortunately, some of the best places for waterfowl to live are on land that people want to use for themselves.

Since waterfowl like to stay near water, many of their best habitats are located in wet areas near the ocean. These wetlands and marshes are wonderful places for many kinds of wildlife. But people often see them as "swamps" that are "no good to anybody" unless they are drained and "developed." So every year, more than *200 thousand acres* of wetlands are destroyed in the United States alone.

In the central United States, there is a splendid place for ducks to hatch their young. It is called the Prairie Pothole area. More than *half* of all ducks hatched in North America each year come from this area. But people are destroying part of the breeding grounds to make room for farms.

Waterfowl habitat in the far north is also in danger. People are looking for oil and minerals in this remote area, and they are already causing pollution of the land and water. All it takes is one large oil spill from a tanker to kill thousands of waterfowl and other birds. As the birds swim in the water, they are coated with oil and poisoned.

But there is a brighter side to the picture. In recent years, some dedicated people have proved that people *can* help. As a result of their efforts, millions of acres of waterfowl habitat have been saved. And scientists have brought some endangered species of waterfowl back from the edge of extinction by using special breeding programs.

In general, we can save waterfowl by doing the same kinds of things that will help save all wild animals. We must leave them enough land for breeding and living. We must be sure they have enough good food. And we must be sure that our machines and chemicals don't harm them.

The Hawaiian geese shown at right are living proof that we can save even the most endangered animals. Thirty years ago, there were only 40 of these beautiful geese alive in the wild. Since then, people have raised thousands of them, and the species is now out of danger.

Index

Index

Art Credits

Page Six: Bottom Left and Right, Trevor Boyer; **Top Right and Left,** Walter Stuart; **Page Seven: Left,** Trevor Boyer; **Right,** Walter Stuart; **Page Eight:** Walter Stuart; **Page Nine: Center,** Trevor Boyer; **Right,** Trevor Boyer; **Pages Ten and Eleven:** Trevor Boyer; **Page Twelve: Center,** Trevor Boyer; **Bottom,** Walter Stuart; **Top Center,** Walter Stuart; **Top Right,** Walter Stuart; **Page Thirteen:** Walter Stuart; **Page Fourteen: Right,** Trevor Boyer; **Left and Bottom,** Walter Stuart; **Page Fifteen:** Walter Stuart.

Photographic Credits

Cover: Wayne Larkiner *(Bruce Coleman, Inc.);* **Pages Four and Five:** Jean-Paul Ferrero *(Ardea London);* **Page Eight: Left,** Med Beauregard *(PPS);* **Right,** Cosmos Blank *(Photo Researchers);* **Page Nine: Top Left,** Frank Todd; **Center Left,** Tom McHugh *(Photo Researchers);* **Bottom,** Frank Todd; **Center Right,** Philippa Scott *(Photo Researchers);* **Uppermost Right,** Frank Todd; **Upper Right,** Joseph Van Wormer *(Bruce Coleman, Inc.);* **Page Twelve: Left,** Calvin Larsen *(Photo Researchers);* **Top Left,** Med Beauregard *(PPS);* **Top Right,** Med Beauregard *(PPS);* **Page Thirteen: Left and Right,** Frank Todd; **Upper Right,** John Shaw *(Tom Stack & Associates);* **Page Fourteen:** Frank Todd; **Page Fifteen: Top Right,** Joseph Van Wormer *(Bruce Coleman, Inc.);* **Middle Left and Middle Right,** Ken Fink *(Bruce Coleman, Inc.);* **Bottom Left,** Joseph Van Wormer *(Bruce Coleman, Inc.);* **Pages Sixteen and Seventeen:** M.D. England *(Ardea Photographers).*

Our Thanks To: Judi Myers *(Sea World, Inc.);* A16 Wilderness Outfitters; Maidhof Brothers Shipware Merchants; Lynnette Wexo; Larry Hoagland *(PPS);* Dann Kunkel.

Creative Education would like to thank Wildlife Education, Ltd., for granting them the rights to print and distribute this hardbound edition.